Workbook Five
Of the Business Essentials
Series

MAXIMISING YOUR
CONVERSION RATES

John Millar

ISBN:153681637X
ISBN-13: 9781536816372

DEDICATION

I dedicate this book to my mother and father, who raised me while self-employed. They taught me to work hard and listen to everyone but to make my own choices as to what is right and what is wrong.. and oh, did I mention work hard?

Anyone who tells you to work smart not hard hasn't ever done it tough and realized that if you work smart AND hard you will achieve more than you can possibly dream.

CONTENTS

PRODUCT DESCRIPTION

Your sales people are your life-blood. You may not like it, but that's the way it is and they are also a breed unto themselves. They don't function like the rest of us – and aren't we glad about that! They have to be tough, negotiating, conciliatory, patient, driven, results-oriented and bloody-minded. If they were not that way, they wouldn't get the results we need to ensure our business grows.

But are you getting the best from them? We tend to respond to our sales staff in one of 2 ways. We either pummel them with our goals and expectations without listening to their input, or we ignore them because we're scared of them. Either way, our business is what suffers as a result. And either way, it's not the team we want or need.

Being immersed in all things business for many years, I have had the opportunity to know sales people very well and these are some of my observations:

- They are, more often than not, motivated by cash and recognition rather than altruistic 'family' values. They want cash, cash, cash and it's their egoistic emphasis is 'me, me, me.'
- They are more mercenary than missionary and don't really give a toss about the philosophies or underlying motives that drive a business. They know why they're there and they just get on with bringing in results.
- They thrive best when they have a solid product to sell, well-defined pricing, a clear quota to aim for and recognizable, clear-cut competitors.
- If they think you don't understand them, they will devise their own methods and approaches that usually end up servicing their needs above yours.

None of these observations renders sales people as 'bad' or immoral or whatever – it simply defines them as results-oriented and task-driven – which is a good thing.

In this Module, we evaluate the best ways in which you can elicit the most profitable results from these amazing people. Understand them. Have them eating out of your business palm and you'll have a wonderfully successful business that has no bounds.

Regards,

John Millar

Today, we're talking about turning prospects in to raving fans and maximizing your conversion rates!

What is a prospect?

A prospect is someone that either takes action like subscribing to your newsletter or most importantly, you collect their details and they have yours.

They haven't bought anything yet but at least we have their details and they have yours.

This is an opportunity for us to be able to engage with that prospect and provide them with some really good quality information. That information can be fairly broad based or generic, and it may in fact be as simple as sending somebody a product catalogue.

We can then go through and assist them through that process and be better quality prospects through our qualification process to make sure that we can identify their specific needs and really get down to the specific product ranges. Once we've done that, we understand their needs and their wants, we then have the opportunity to niche our offering to them and make sure that it's specific and based on what they need, and what they should

---

So what is SALES?

Sales is merely identifying and satisfying a customer's needs and wants profitably.

What are your top three words that you'd like to use when you think of the word "salesman"?

Good quality sales people are dedicated to helping other people to achieve their needs and wants profitably for all parties and in the most professional way possible.

Lets' have a look at the four most common types of sales people.

First of all, you've got the "order taker."

All they're really doing is sitting back waiting for someone to say, "Oh excuse me, can I actually buy that please?"

This is the shop assistant who sits behind the counter waiting for you to bring them what you want them to put through the register. They may have acknowledged you on the way in, they may even have made half an attempt to see if they can assist you, but they haven't really done it well. If they had, then they wouldn't be in this category which is just simply the order taker.

The second one is the "product pusher."

They don't do anything else but talk about how the product is going to suit you. They're convinced their product is great and whether or not you want or need it they are going to do all they can to sell it to you.

The third type is the "over seller."

They promise the world just to get the sale. They promise everything and give very little. In fact, it's one of the biggest problems that create buyer's remorse. They sold something to somebody and they've offered things and made promises and made perhaps illusions towards the achievement of things that never actually occur. Too often the over seller just keeps pushing, and pushing until you either take what they are trying to flog you or you get away from this toxic individual

The fourth one is my favorite, the "problem solver."

The problem solver really wants to find out what the customer needs and wants. They ask a lot of questions. If they are on a one on one appointment with a particular prospect and they are both having a cup of coffee and the reality is they will have finished their coffee before the prospect has because they have only spoken to ask more questions to better understand what is needed to achieve the best result together. Selling by definition, is all about identifying and satisfying a customer's needs

You must make sure that you can actually sell by keeping up to date with quality training, reading and professional development activities.

What are the three beliefs that you hold to be true when you say the word "customers"?

1.
....

2.
....

3.
....
....

> Sales decisions are actually made on two different levels. They're made justified logic but they're made with emotion.

....
....
....
....
....
....

> They need the reasons buy on emotion and the facts to justify with logic.

Let's think about beliefs around money. There's nothing wrong with profit!

Money is nothing more than an idea backed with confidence.

....
....
....
....
....
....
....
....

If you want sales and to instill confidence in everything that you do you must focus on your communication.

True communication is the response that you get.
If you don't get the answer that you want, you need to ask a better question.

There are three major modes for when communicating with people.

1. The first is the words that we use
2. The second is through the use of our voice when we deliver those words
3. The third is your body language

Only 7 percent of what we say (the words we use) have impact

38 percent is the voice that we use; the pitch, the pace, the timbre, the volume that we use, the way that we express those words A massive 55 percent of all communication is non-verbal (body language).

The whole idea is that unless you present yourself in a confident manner, it's not likely to inspire and instill confidence from others.
It's all about matching and mirroring but not mimicking.

....

....

....

....

....

What are the modalities of communication?

They are visual, auditory and kinesthetic.
Everybody learns and everyone communicates very differently!

....

....

....

....

Approximately 40 percent of the population works very heavily towards a visual modality, around 20 percent from auditory, and another 40 percent which is really from the kinesthetic modality.

If you said something to me like, "I can hear what you're saying. That sounds right to me." Then you know what, I'm probably speaking to somebody who uses auditory styles of communication.

If someone says "Look, I see what you mean. That looks spot on to me." Then I'm probably talking about somebody who's more of a visual modality.

If somebody turned and said "Well that feels good. I feel pretty solid about that idea." Then that person wants to be communicated in the mode of the kinesthetic modality.

The DISC model is simple and elegant when looking at behavioral and attitudinal sides of people alongside the modality of their learning and communication.

A high "D" or high dominant would be a bull
A high "I" is a peacock.
The high "S" is the sympathetic lamb
The high "C," is known as conscientious as an Owl

These all make up the DISC profile

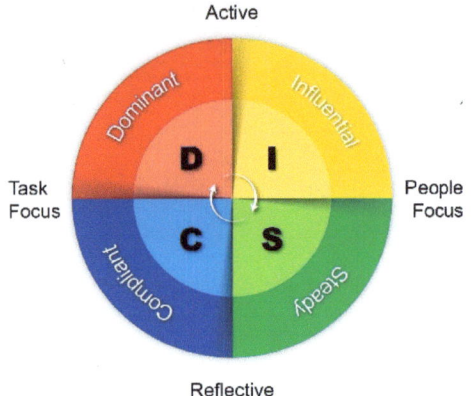

Unless you and your sales person, believe that what you're offering is truly great value then asking for an investment will across as false and insincere.

Always get agreement to move forward or take particular action and then getting their permission to stay in contact with them or to ask them for their business and for their referrals.

- What's the purpose statement in your business?

- What are the questions that you need to ask your clients to understand their needs?

- When dealing with your clients are you always fully present and in the moment with them?

"I would suggest that if you are telling, you are not selling."

Sales is all about making a change. It's about moving your clients from one state to another. This change of state may simply be moving them from not owning your product and service to owning it.

Sales is all about making a change. It's about moving your clients from one state to another. This change of state may simply be moving them from not owning your product and service to owning it.

Closing a sale shouldn't be a crunch at the end, it is a natural culmination of the process that reaches the stage where they start asking new questions, asking the buying questions that you need to hear to give you permission to progress. Things like "how soon can I get that? What colors is that available in? Are there any other options that are available with that? If I order that now what time could   be delivered?"

Ask lots and lots of questions

Old selling versus the new selling

In the old style of selling we would spend very little time on building rapport, we'd spend an enormous amount of time trying to sell and crunch the deal, and then we'd spend a little bit of time in follow up.

New selling is very, very different. We spend a lot more time building rapport, understanding and appreciation of them and their needs. We spend very little time in the actual selling because now they've told everything they'd like to buy and why, and we're just helping them to achieve those things. Then after the sale experience, whether they've purchased or not, we spend an enormous amount of time following up

----

We want to see them again. We want their referral business. We want their repeat business. We want them to come back for the other things that revolve around the products and services that we have.

We need to ask lots of open-ended questions.

An open-ended question is one by which that cannot be answered with a yes or a no. It's a question that must be answered with a full answer.

A closed-ended question is literally one that you may want to ask that when you want a yes or a no because that's part of the tie-down process.

I like to ask permission when I ask questions

I'm genuinely asking people questions because I really want to help them and if I can't understand where they're coming from completely and fully then how can I expect to help them?

....

....

....

....

....

What are the common questions that you need to ask to best understand how to help you question and to help your clients?

1. ....

2. ....

3. ....

4. ....

5. ....

What are the questions that are going to help you to understand whether or not this is the real prospect and whether or not this prospect is somebody that you can help?

1. ....

2. ....

3. ....

4. ....

5. ....

If you don't dig in hard and dig in deep and understand fully, you may waste a lot of your time and theirs!

Most people don't like to make decisions and sometimes you need to help them to do so.

Remember an objection can be a couple of things. One, it can be their way of saying, "Please help me to understand or overcome these things so that I can purchase your product and services." Two, it can be reluctance to make a decision. Most of us are raised as children not make decisions quickly. Three it can sometimes just come down to fear, that fear of change and that fear of actually doing something FEAR – False

"W" is for welcoming their objections.
"R" is Repeat the objection back to them.
"I" is for isolate the objection so nothing sneaks back on you later.
"O" is overcome the objection.

A few more things to consider:

Ask questions in a way that you'd like to be asked those questions.

- Always be on time
- Keep in touch throughout the sales process
- Do some research on what your clients REALLY need and want
- Get lots of written and video testimonials.
- Always follow up.
- Do something a little bit different.
- Be consistent, if you're not consistent then you are nothing.
- Looking at the ladder of loyalty

RAVING FAN

ADVOCATE
MEMBER
CLIENT
CUSTOMER
PROSPECT
SUSPECT

The first is the "shopper stage," at the shopper stage they've actually parted with some hard earned cash with us.

Sit down and create a list of questions that is your question funnel. Work on your purpose statement for you and your sales team.

Create a sales kit.

What are the things that you are going to do to make sure that you

Believe in yourself and what you do and it will come across.

Thank you very much and I'll see you next time!

John Millar

Business Essentials Series...

Disc 1 in the Business Essentials Series
Gaining Focus in Your Business

This is about your fundamental learning skills and what you will need to do to change them to vastly improve the way you look
at your development to become a truly effective business owner not just simply remain self-employed.

You will also give you some excellent tools to set goals, work on your plans and create a diary that will allow you to steal your time back to begin moving your business from chaos to control.

Disc 2 in the Business Essentials Series
Getting Your Financials Right

You will learn the importance of understanding your financials.

After all being in business is about making profit and having cash flow work for YOU since you are responsible for your profits.
Become your accountant and book keepers best friend by understanding more about how the financials in your business works so you can ask them better questions to maximise your profits not simply ensure tax compliance.

Disc 3 in the Business Essentials Series
Leveraging Your Business Harder

You will learn the principles of what and how to leverage far more in your business to get more from less and to work far smarter and not just harder.

Here is where you will receive some of the tools you will need to better understand how to get your business flying, what it is you need to test and measure, how to do it and WHY it's so important.

Disc 4 in the Business Essentials Series
How to Generate More Clients Profitably

This is where you will determine your uniqueness, develop a meaningful guarantee and learn the basics of good advertising.

You will gain a better appreciation between the difference of Marketing and Advertising, learn how to get the most for the least investment and ensure that you do it all profitably.

Disc 5 in the Business Essentials Series
Maximising Your Conversion Rates

Get to know how your Sales Pipeline REALLY works and how to identify who your suspects really are, convert prospects into regular shoppers and understand how much more work you can do to maximise your sales experience.

Disc 6 in the Business Essentials Series
Meet and Exceed Your Clients Expectations

Now you have new customers, how do you make sure you KEEP them, how do you wanting to come back time and again while telling their friends? ...this is where you really make a difference.

Disc 7 in the Business Essentials Series

Systemising Your Business For Consistent Excellence

Do you recognise the importance of having systems in your business and how they can improve your profitability?

We show you how to systemise like a corporate while retaining the culture of a smaller business. Understanding how we systemise for routine and humanise for the exceptions will enable you to be the best in your field every time.

Disc 8 in the Business Essentials Series

Do You Have a Champion Team with a Champion Leader?

This is about having the right people on the bus. It starts with you however so you'll learn how to maximise your own skills and then you will attract and retain the right people.

When you understand how the TEAM is the most important part of your business and what needs to be done to achieve the very best from yourselves and others you are well on your way to becoming a better manager of this invaluable resource.

Disc 9 in the Business Essentials Series

The Essentials of Getting Your Time Back.

This is where you get to redefine your time management You will understand better how you can start working far more on the business than in the business than ever before.

You will also finally find out why others can seem to fit more into their day while having a great LIFE – WORK balance (notice the order!)..

Disc 10 in the Business Essentials Series

Simply Brilliant Customer Service.

It's so easy to give mediocre or good customer service but it's just as easy to give amazing service to your customers and delight them.

You will understand the simple easy steps that you must take to provide consistently brilliant service and how to get your team excited about doing it.

Disc 11 in the Business Essentials Series

Discovering DISC and EQ not just IQ.

We believe for things to change first you must change so here you will learn why you behave as you do and just as importantly understand why other people react and act the way they do.

You will also learn what DISC really is and what it isn't. You will learn how to apply these important principles in your recruitment and team management / development.

You will learn how to use these ideas in creating a more dynamic team and discover the what and why of emotional intelligence. You will also develop key strategies for using the knowledge here and the tools we have available on our website and why we place such a massive emphasis on DISC and other tools that support, train and develop your team.

You will also learn how to use these skills and observations at home and socially not just at the workplace.

Disc 12 in the Business Essentials Series
Quality Recruitment.
Recruitment of the right people for the right reasons in the right roles for your team is so incredibly important yet so often ignored or pushed to the rear.

You will learn who the right person is for your business and the role you want filled.
You will be able to identify the right people early in the process to save yourself and them the time and money wasted with antique recruitment methodologies that just don't work anymore.

How to get the best out of your recruitment activities so you can keep the assets you acquire for the long term and get the best return from your investment.

ABOUT THE AUTHOR

John Millar is the Managing Director, Senior Business Coach Trainer and Consultant with More Profit Less Time Pty Ltd and CEO-ONDEMAND. Along with his many other business interests, John is proud to have been an associate of the most successful coaching team in the world.

He is recognized as a global leader and has been benchmarked against over 1,300 colleagues in 31 countries. John has over 25 years of hands-on ownership, management, coaching, and entrepreneurial experience in a broad range of industry sectors, including retail, wholesale, import, export, IT, trades and trade services, automotive, primary production, food services, transport, manufacturing, mining, professional services, the fitness industry, and more.

He has extensive experience developing and providing training for small to medium-sized companies and a variety of publicly listed corporate companies. John is an accomplished and talented public and professional speaker. He has been a mentor working with sales/management activities for businesses with a turnover under $100,000 per annum, over $100 million turnover, and everything in between, with great success.

John currently works with business owners and their teams across Australia and has a "Whatever it takes" attitude that has enabled him to help his clients grow their business profits by up to 800%.

 If you are ready to be coached by one of the best in the business, register at:

www.ceo-ondemand.com.au

Make sure to visit www.moreprofitlesstime.com for the new online Management Development Program: The Business Essentials Series.

ACCLAIM FOR JOHN MILLAR'S
Business Coaching and Training in their own words...

"Without John Millar as my Business Coach I wouldn't have a business today."—Grant Jennings Managing Director, Jigsaw Projects

"Taking the decision to be coached and trained by John Millar was carefully considered after experiencing those who over promised and under delivered. I am pleased to say the content of his courses are the tools we all need to master as business owners. His delivery is engaging, thought provoking and empowering and after every session l came away re-energised. John always makes himself available for business building advice both via Skype and face to face beyond the scope of delivery. With his extensive personal experience in building small businesses, he knows and understands what it takes to establish and grow a business. I have no hesitation endorsing John Millar as an educator and business coach and the bonus is he is a very nice person."—Anne Lederman Managing Director FB Salons"

Johns training with my management team was excellent, it was very different from the business coaching and support I have had in the past. John was clear, thoughtful and he addressed the issues we needed to cover without us even knowing they were being addressed! His follow up has been fantastic and exactly what I needed. I would recommend John and his team to anyone looking at getting some business coaching and training done" —Wendy Crawford, Peopleworx

"In my dealings with John as our business coach, I have found him to be a motivated and insightful agent of positive change. He is able to burrow down to the root cause of issues and introduce effective forms of measurement. John then identifies and implements practical solutions and is there to provide the gentle persuasion required to ensure that results are achieved." —Mark Felton, Lindale Insurances

"You have coached and trained us so well throughout the year that we are now used to & find it easy to prepare a 90 day plan, then breaks it down to actionable bite size pieces. Planning in business & personal life certainly is important. It allows us to identify the important things & the bigger picture. Thank you for your support & guidance throughout the year. And not to mention your insight, external perspective to review & assist our business moving forward." —Linda Turner, Director Roy A McDonald Certified Practicing Accountants

"If you want to achieve sales results you never thought were possible and give yourself a competitive edge my strong suggestion is to engage John services and listen closely to what John has to say, during the time I was trained by John I was one of eight sales consultants in a national business for 10 out of the 13 months I lead the sales tally and in 1 quarter I generated three times the revenue of the national sales force combined. Johns training and experience was well worth the investment and paid big dividends. Thanks John." —Julian Fadini, Bellvue Capital

"John is a very enthusiastic trainer and business coach, he is very passionate about getting business owners and their team where they need to be. He goes the extra mile to keep ahead of the latest developments which he then uses to benefit his clients." —Darren Reddy CPA

"I have been to a few seminars and heard John speak numerous times about sales, marketing and business. He is a very knowledgeable and extremely enthusiastic business coach in all his interactions and I would recommend him to all business owners who need a sales and marketing boost!" —Andrew Heath, Managing Director, Fresh Living Group

"I worked with John Millar and found his business knowledge, passion and innovation to be inspiring. He has always been able to set (and achieve) strategic long and short-term goals both for himself and his clients without losing that personal connection he builds with everyone he meets. He has been and I believe will continue to be a strong mentor and trainer for anyone wanting to take that next step in their business." —Bree Webster, Online Marketing Guru

"Massive Action Day" – what an understatement, John Millars 4 hour frenzy challenged me to seriously review areas of my business I would not have gone to .... In this way, the process identified incongruence's in my mind, my business and my modus operandi. It's created a paradigm shift. Thanks John, the road map just got a whole lot clearer. Your friendship and insights since 2003 have been a gift to my business and I." —Andrew Reay, Counsellor, Hypnotherapist and Counsellor, Thinkshift Transformations

"John Millar is not your usual Business coach or trainer; he gets involved with you and your business and provides hands on help to make sure you follow through on his advice. He is highly motivated to help his clients and his personal guarantee certainly shows this. He has now transposed his thoughts, advice and love of good business onto a series of DVD's in his business venture – More Profit Less Time. This has excellent tips and advice for anyone either starting out or already in business. I highly recommend John to any business owner who wants to run a business and not a j.o.b.!" —Darren Cassidy, Managing Director HR2U

"I and many of my Business Partners and colleagues have worked with John since 2010 as our business oath, trainer and motivator and found him to be an extremely motivational person to assist us achieve our business goals. This company and its products allows for John's skill set to be accessed by a wider number of potential clients. His very professional DVD series is extremely good value for money and is easily accessible for all of us who are time poor. If you are looking to maximise your and your business's results and to start achieving your goals and dreams, contact John; you won't look back!!" —Mark Cleland, Mortgage Choice

"John develops real relationships with the people he comes into contact with. He is pasionate about what he does. His DVD and group training series, is full of good ideas and process to make your business better. Knowing what to do and actually doing it are two different things. John is excellent at helping you get things done." —Carey Rudd, Sales Director, Online Knowledge

"I have known John since 2004 and found him to be extremely knowledgably in both Sales and Business systems as a business coach without peer. John has provided me with business advice as well as personal coaching over the years, helping me with the running of my organisation. I'm impressed with John's DVD series where he has condensed a lot of the information in an easy to follow format that any business owner can use immediately. I wish he had released these DVDs earlier, as they are a goldmine of information, and practical how to that allow anyone to increase the profit in their business and get back valuable wasted time." —Steve Psaradellis, Managing Director, TEBA

"John's DVD and workbook delivery of his no-nonsense advice provides a low-cost option for those business owners looking to set and achieve goals that will increase profit. I found the conversational style of the DVD's easy to follow, whilst the requirement to pause the DVD and write down some action points ensured a level of commitment to the advice being provided." — Mark Felton, Lindale Insurances

"I only met John briefly at a BNI meeting and knew instantly i need to hire him for my business as my business coach. His attitude towards work and how to improve my cash line had an instant effect on before, even before I finally hired him on an official basis. I found myself thinking "what would John do" and this was only after just meeting him. I cannot see my business expend and give me "More Profit Less Time" without John's expert direction and training. If you want to succeed in business life, you need John Millar, without him you're just kidding yourself " —Leslie Cachia, Managing Director, Letac Drafting

"I can highly recommend John Millar to any business owner who wants to grow his business. When I hear very positive feedback from colleagues who are skeptics by nature about John's ability and skills, I know John will help all those he comes in contact with. John comes with a selfless nature and the willingness to work inside a client's business to make it succeed. Rare indeed!" —Darren Cassidy, Managing Director, HR2U "I first met John Millar in mid-2010 and have always found him to be of an honest and generous character that engenders an easy association with him. I love how easy he is to listen to and how passionate he is about his work and topics. John demonstrates a love for life and his work and I have no hesitation in recommending his services." —Kathie M Thomas, Managing Director, VA

"I have listened to John speak on a number of occasions and find him a very knowledgeable speaker with a passion for what he does. I have also interacted with a number of his clients and they all tell me that he helps them achieve results in their business. If you are looking for business help John is a person you can trust." —Carey Rudd, Sales Director, Online Knowledge

"John knows his stuff, he knows how the get results, John has so many great ideas in building a business and helping business owners work less and make more money. John has released a DVD set on doing just that. I have watched the 1st one and it was great, very informative and easy to understand, I happily recommend John to anyone in need of help and guidance" —Frank Eramo, Proprietor, Dynotune

"I have known John only for a short time, however the impact that he has had on me, not just my business has helped me to visualise opportunities that I began to doubt my ability to realise. He is encouraging and at the same time challenging so that he can/you can, begin to see how to maximise the business potential, John calls it being an unreasonable friend, I call it being a mate. If you have any questions about the direction of your business, if you want to seem your bottom line improve not just turnover but real profit, if you want a person who will work with you then I strongly recommend that you engage him at your earliest convenience. John is the best thing that has happened to my business. I could tell you about the way he is on track to make 1/2 a million for me on his contacts alone, but that actually sells him short, he has become like my partner in business, and cares about my success as if it was his own, we will flourish because I took the step to employ his training to help me grow. If you get a chance to get him training you, don't wait like I did, get in as quickly as possible, his time is your business and if like me your business is to make money, then every day you don't have him on retainer you lose money." —Russell Summers, Managing Director, The Give Life Centre

"It's usually easy to be mediocre in business but it's impossible when you have John Millar training you. He has been my right hand since 2003!" —David Manser, CFO, Hydrosteer

"I now have a commercial, profitable business and now it's my choice when I work IN my business and when I work ON it and have had john helping me in business since 1988. I can't imagine not having John as a part of our business." —David Wall, Director, D&K Transport

"The work John has done since 2008 coaching and training our marketing team, administration and finance teams, buyers, store managers and staff nationally have been fantastic." —Ross Sudano, Director, Anaconda Adventure Stores

"John is a creative, professional, practical and committed business coach and trainer. His approach since we first met him in 1994 to working with a client team through the application of useful tools, information and anecdotes along with his easy going & easy to understand delivery sets him apart from other business coaches that I have used in the past." —Anthony Beasley, Director, The Astra Group

"I have worked with John Millar for the since 2004 and I didn't think it was possible to achieve what we have achieved together. His business coaching, training and services just get better and better!" —Terrance Chong, Managing Director, Echo Graphics and Printing

"John's business coaching, training and support has transformed our business across Australia and New Zealand since 2008."—Rose Vis, Managing Director, VIP Australia

"We first met John in 2005, he is AMAZING at sales, marketing, operations, logistics, finance training and so much more. Since engaging John as our business coach our business has exploded, our team are happy, our clients are raving about us and my husband and I now take at least 12 weeks holidays a year, EVERY year." —Shirley Du, Director, Goldline Technology

"It's the no nonsense results driven business coaching and training focus John bought to the table that had such a massive effect on our business." —David Runkel, Director, Tracomp Fabrication and Steel

"We started working with John in early 2010, within 90 days of working with and being trained by John Millar we had the biggest and most profitable month in our 15 year history. That's impressive." —Hugh Gilchrist, Managing Director, Australian Moulding Company

"If you don't have John as your business trainer you aren't meeting your business potential." —Don Robertson, Director, Medallion Electrical Services

Thank You